ZOMBIE ZONE

Zombies
Through the Ages

by Ruth Owen

Consultant: Luke W. Boyd
Editor in Chief
Zombie Research Society
Los Angeles, California

BEARPORT
PUBLISHING

New York, New York

Credits

Cover, © Zacarias Pereira da Mata/Shutterstock, © Gergely Zsolnai/Shutterstock, and © Y Photo Studio/ Shutterstock; 3L, © froe_mic/Shutterstock; 4–5, © Kim Jones; 6, © Alex Tihonovs/Shutterstock; 7L, © Luchiiiya/Shutterstock; 7R, © Smit/Shutterstock; 8B, © Armands Pharyos/Alamy; 8–9, © Creative Travel Projects/Shutterstock, © Igor Zh/Shutterstock, © Tereshchenko Dmitry/Shutterstock, and © Capture Light/ Shutterstock; 10, © Andrey Popov/Shutterstock and © Julia Sudnitskaya/Shutterstock; 11T, © Pavel Svoboda Photography/Shutterstock; 11B, © Qrt/Alamy; 12–13, © Kim Jones; 14, © redhumv/Istock Photo; 15T, © Anyka/ Alamy; 15L, © mauritius images GmbH/Alamy; 15R, © Mariia Suvorova/Shutterstock; 16L, © Eye of Science/ Science Photo Library; 16R, © tsuneomp/Shutterstock; 17TL, © Eric Isselee/Shutterstock; 17TR, © ASK Images/Alamy; 17B, © spline x/Shutterstock; 18L, © timquo/Shutterstock; 18R, © Moviestore Collection Ltd/ Alamy; 19, © Collection Christophel/Alamy; 20, © Matthew Horwood/Alamy; 21TL, © Shane Aurousseau/ Alamy; 21TR, © RugliG/Shutterstock; 21B, © Ben Romalis/Shutterstock; 22T, © rukxstockphoto/Shutterstock; 22C, © Ruth Owen; 22R, © Luis Louro/Shutterstock.

Publisher: Kenn Goin
Senior Editor: Joyce Tavolacci
Creative Director: Spencer Brinker
Photo Researcher: Ruth Owen Books

Library of Congress Cataloging-in-Publication Data

Names: Owen, Ruth, 1967– author.
Title: Zombies through the ages / by Ruth Owen.
Description: New York : Bearport Publishing Company, Inc., 2018. | Series:
    Zombie zone | Includes bibliographical references and index.
Identifiers: LCCN 2017047846 (print) | LCCN 2017056184 (ebook) |
  ISBN 9781684025008 (Ebook) | ISBN 9781684024421 (library)
Subjects: LCSH: Zombies—Juvenile literature.
Classification: LCC GR581 (ebook) | LCC GR581 .O95 2018 (print) | DDC
    398.21—dc23
LC record available at https://lccn.loc.gov/2017047846

For more information, write to Bearport Publishing Company, Inc., 45 West 21st Street, Suite 3B, New York, New York 10010. Printed in the United States of America.

10 9 8 7 6 5 4 3 2 1

Contents

A Tale of the Undead

It was around the year 1090 in the tiny English village of Drakelow. One evening at sunset, two men were walking through the village. They were very pale and their clothes were torn and dirty. Even stranger, they were carrying wooden **coffins** on their backs.

When the villagers saw the odd figures, they froze with **terror**. Earlier that day, those same men had been buried in the local cemetery as lifeless **corpses**!

The people of Drakelow knew there could be only one explanation—the men had become **revenants**. They were now evil corpses that rise from their graves each night to terrorize the living!

The word *revenant* comes from the French word *revenir*, which means "to return." Today, a corpse that has come back to life is usually known as a zombie.

The Revenants Return!

The following night, the revenants crawled from their graves once again. They used their coffins to bang on houses where the villagers lived. The terrified people hid. They knew that any person who came in contact with the evil corpses would get the **plague** and die.

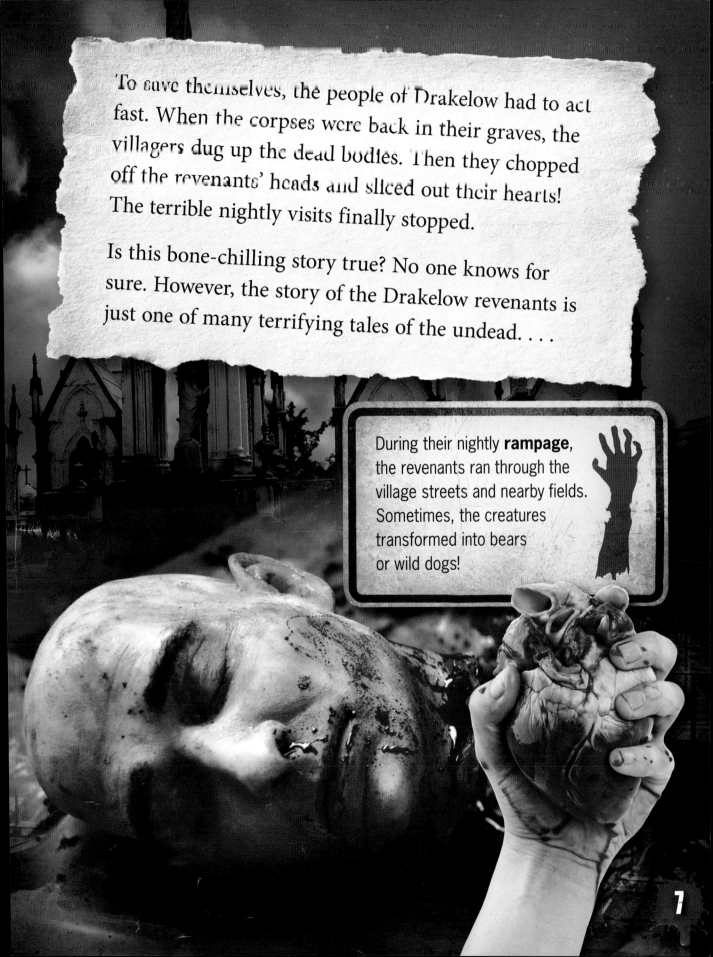

To save themselves, the people of Drakelow had to act fast. When the corpses were back in their graves, the villagers dug up the dead bodies. Then they chopped off the revenants' heads and sliced out their hearts! The terrible nightly visits finally stopped.

Is this bone-chilling story true? No one knows for sure. However, the story of the Drakelow revenants is just one of many terrifying tales of the undead. . . .

During their nightly **rampage**, the revenants ran through the village streets and nearby fields. Sometimes, the creatures transformed into bears or wild dogs!

Deadly Draugrs

More than 1,000 years ago, the Viking people of northern Europe told their own horrifying tales of the walking dead. They believed that the corpse of a warrior could rise from its grave as a deadly *draugr*.

According to Viking legend, a draugr's skin was *hel-blár*, which means "as black as death" in the Norse language. The creature would reek of **decay**, and its body could swell to the size of an ox. A draugr was able to change form, becoming a gray horse with a broken back or a skinned bull. It was so strong it could easily crush the bones of a human.

One type of draugr would guard its **burial mound**, which was filled with weapons and treasure. Anybody who dared to steal from the grave would be **slaughtered**—and eaten!

Viking burial mound

Viking graves were often covered with a mound of rocks.

A picture of what a Viking draugr might look like

A draugr might also change into a cat and sit on the chest of a sleeping person. The cat would grow heavier and heavier until its victim **suffocated**!

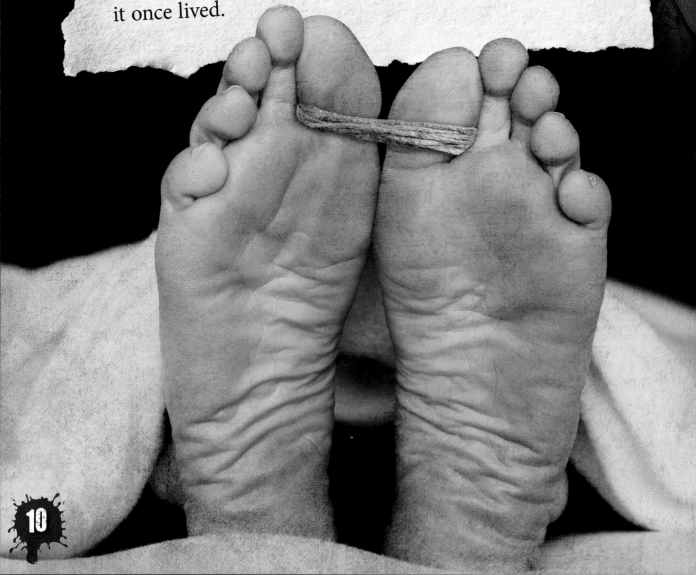

An Unwelcome Visitor

To prevent a dead warrior from becoming a draugr, the Viking people did some unusual things. For example, they would tie a corpse's big toes together so it couldn't walk. Sharp needles might also be pushed into the soles of the dead warrior's feet.

The Vikings worried that if the ties and needles didn't work, a draugr might try to return to the house where it once lived.

Vikings also believed the creature could only re-enter its home the same way its corpse had left. So, to keep a corpse from returning home, people would carry the dead body out through a small hole in the wall of the house. Then the hole, also known as a corpse door, would be blocked. That way, if a draugr tried to return home, it would not be able to get inside.

Replicas of Viking houses

One way to destroy a draugr was for a living warrior to cut off the creature's head and burn it. After its second death, the draugr would be gone forever.

A Viking skull

Tibetan Ro-Langs

In the country of Tibet, it's believed that zombielike creatures walk the earth. According to Tibetan **folklore**, if an evil spirit enters a corpse, it comes back to life as a *ro-langs*. It's also believed that **sorcerers** can create a ro-langs to gain magical powers.

To do this, a sorcerer takes hold of a dead body. Then he places his lips to the corpse's mouth. As the sorcerer chants into the corpse, the body comes back to life as a ro-langs. The undead creature grows stronger and stronger, but the sorcerer must not let go or he will be killed.

Finally, the ro-langs sticks out its tongue, and the sorcerer bites it off! This causes the ro-langs to die. The sorcerer keeps the ro-langs's tongue, which gives him special powers.

A ro-langs can turn a living person into the undead just by laying the palm of its hand on a person's head.

13

Voodoo Zombies

For hundreds of years, people on the Caribbean island of Haiti have lived in fear of becoming a zombie. Their belief in the undead comes from a religion called **voodoo**. It's said that evil voodoo sorcerers, called bokors, can turn people into zombies.

The voodoo religion can be traced back to Africa. The word *zombie* may be formed from the words *ndzumbi*, meaning "corpse," and *nzambi*, which means "spirit of a dead person." These words come from two different African languages.

Some say a bokor kills a victim using a powder that contains poison and ground-up human bones. Once the corpse is in its grave, the bokor digs up the body. Using magic, the bokor then brings the dead body back to life.

It's believed that a bokor turns a person into a zombie to work as a slave. To control the undead creature, the bokor feeds it a special food called zombie cucumber.

Human thigh bones

A grave in Haiti

Fact or Fiction?

People have lived in fear of zombies for hundreds of years. Are **supernatural** forces at work? Or could there be a scientific explanation for the living dead?

In the past, people in **comas** who appeared dead were sometimes buried alive. If the person then woke up from the coma and crawled from his or her grave, it would look as if a corpse had returned from the dead.

Hundreds of years ago, people did not know that diseases are caused by germs. If someone touched a diseased corpse, he or she may have become ill. So, it appeared as if the dead could make the living sick!

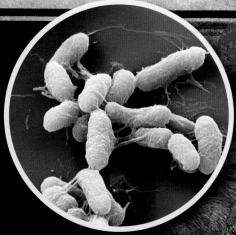

This image was taken with a powerful microscope. It shows the germs that cause bubonic plague, or Black Death.

In Haiti, scientists have examined whether bokors really can create zombies. One theory is that the powder made by bokors contains a powerful poison that comes from puffer fish. This poison can paralyze a victim, making the person seem dead. Once the poison's effects wear off, however, it could appear as if the corpse has come back to life. Scientists have also investigated zombie cucumber, which is the fruit of the poisonous datura plant. Eating this fruit could make a person so sick, he or she would behave like a mindless zombie.

Puffer fish liver

A puffer fish's liver is one of the most poisonous parts of the fish.

Puffer fish

A datura or zombie cucumber plant

Rise of the Flesh-Eaters

In modern times, a new kind of zombie fills us with fear and dread—flesh-eaters! Flesh-eating zombies first appeared in a 1968 movie called *Night of the Living Dead*, created by filmmaker George Romero.

In the film, corpses rise from their graves to attack and feed on the living. A group of people becomes trapped in a **remote** farmhouse. They fight to survive, but one by one, they are eaten . . . or become zombies themselves! Although the movie was black and white, it horrified—and excited—many moviegoers. The flesh-eating zombie craze had begun!

Zombie movies and TV shows use fake body parts, such as this rubber hand.

Zombies from *Night of the Living Dead*

Today, there are countless zombie movies and TV shows. Millions of people tune in to watch the TV show *The Walking Dead*, which is based on a comic book series of the same name. In each episode, survivors of a **zombie apocalypse** try to avoid being attacked by undead creatures known as "walkers."

A crowd of walkers and a human survivor from *The Walking Dead*

The actors who play zombies in *The Walking Dead* go to special classes, or zombie school, to learn how to move and act like a zombie!

Obsessed with Zombies!

The thought of coming face-to-face with a zombie terrifies most people—but not everyone!

Imagine a group of old, abandoned buildings. You step into a maze of empty hallways and shadowy rooms. Your mission—to survive a zombie attack! Sound like fun? Some companies, like NYZ Apocalypse, stage zombie survival games, in which fans can experience what it's like to be hunted by the walking dead.

An actor from a zombie game called *2.8 Hours Later* in Cardiff, South Wales

In cities around the world, zombie lovers also dress up as corpses and join zombie walks! At some events more than 20,000 groaning, blood-splattered zombies stagger through city streets.

Could zombies actually threaten humankind in the future? The unsettling question remains. . . .

Zombie fans wear fun costumes and gruesome make-up to take part in zombie walks.

At the Brisbane Zombie Walk in Australia, the participants raise money for research into brain diseases and injuries. Brains, after all, are zombies' favorite food!

A tasty meal for a zombie? No. Just a delicious brain-shaped cake for a zombie fan!

21

Make Zombie Blood

If you're dressing as a zombie for Halloween or a zombie walk, you'll need plenty of blood for your costume. This homemade blood recipe looks great—and actually tastes good!

How to Make Fake Blood:

1. Put 4 teaspoons of corn syrup and 1 teaspoon of flour in a bowl and mix thoroughly.

Measuring spoon

2. Add a small dab of red food coloring (about half the size of a pea) to the mixture and stir. Add more red coloring, if needed, to get a bright-red color.

3. To make dark-red blood, dip a toothpick into the blue food coloring and stir into the mixture. You will only need a tiny amount of blue to darken the blood.

Blue food coloring

4. Smear the sticky blood over your skin and costume. You can smear it around your mouth to make it look as if you've been feasting on brains!

You will need:

- Measuring spoons
- Corn syrup
- Flour
- A bowl
- Red and blue gel food coloring
- A small spoon for mixing
- A toothpick

⚠ **BE CAREFUL!**

Some food colorings can cause staining. Only wear old clothes, or check if the blood will stain by testing it on a small piece of fabric before adding it to your costume.

Glossary

burial mound (BER-ee-uhl MOUND) a large mound of soil above a grave

coffins (KAWF-inz) long boxes in which dead bodies are buried

comas (KOH-muhz) states in which a person is unconscious and cannot wake up

corpses (KORPS-iz) dead bodies

decay (di-KAY) the breaking down or rotting of something

folklore (FOHK-lawr) traditional beliefs and stories

plague (PLAYG) a deadly disease that spreads quickly, such as the bubonic plague

rampage (RAM-payj) a period of violent and destructive behavior

remote (ri-MOHT) far from a town or city

revenants (REV-uh-nuhnts) people who have returned from the dead, usually by climbing out of their graves

slaughtered (SLAW-terd) killed violently

sorcerers (SOR-sur-erz) people who are believed to have magical powers

suffocated (SUHF-uh-kay-tid) killed by having one's supply of air stopped

supernatural (soo-pur-NACH-ur-uhl) having to do with something that breaks the laws of nature

terror (TER-uhr) extreme fear

voodoo (VOO-doo) a religion that includes some traditional African beliefs

zombie apocalypse (ZOM-bee uh-POK-uh-lips) a terrible disaster in which zombies kill millions of people

Index

Read More

Goldsworthy, Steve. *Zombies: The Truth Behind History's Terrifying Flesh-Eaters (Monster Handbooks)*. North Mankato, MN: Capstone (2015).

Marsico, Katie. *Undead Monsters: From Mummies to Zombies (Monster Mania)*. Minneapolis, MN: Lerner (2017).

Owen, Ruth. *Becoming a Zombie (Zombie Zone)*. New York: Bearport (2018).

Learn More Online

To learn more about zombies through the ages, visit
www.bearportpublishing.com/ZombieZone

About the Author

Ruth Owen has been developing and writing children's books for more than 10 years. She lives in Cornwall, England, just minutes from the ocean. If there's a zombie apocalypse, she intends to escape by boat!